Breaking Through

The Winning Mindset of 20 Athletes Who
Overcame Challenges and Adversity to Become
Sports Heroes

Hannah Blake

Please join our mailing list for updates and information about other upcoming books by Hannah Blake.

hannah blake

Table of Contents

JIM ABBOTT

Overcoming the Odds with
Adaptation and Optimism

Jim Abbott's journey is a powerful story of determination, innovation, and heart. Born without a right hand, Abbott defied all odds to become a successful Major League Baseball pitcher. His path—from a small town in Michigan to the grand stage of professional baseball—shows us that with creativity and relentless optimism, even the most significant challenges can become steppingstones. More than just a great athlete, Jim inspired people worldwide by showing what's possible when you believe in yourself.

A Childhood Challenge

Jim Abbott was born in Flint, Michigan, on September 19, 1967. From the start, life presented him with a challenge—he was born without his right hand. But what could have been a lifelong barrier instead became the beginning of an incredible story.

Jim's parents, Mike and Kathy, were his biggest supporters. They didn't treat him like he was limited. Instead, they encouraged independence and taught him how to adapt. They believed that a physical difference should never stop someone from living a whole and active life.

From a young age, Jim loved sports. He especially loved playing catch with his dad in the backyard. He figured out his unique way to play baseball: he balanced the glove on his right arm, threw the ball with his left hand, and then quickly slid his glove back to field the ball. This creative method became his signature move and showed his ability to adapt and problem-solve like a true athlete.

Chasing the Dream

In high school at Flint Central, Jim didn't just play—he stood out. He became a star in both baseball and football. Though some people doubted him, he worked hard and quickly proved that he belonged on the field.

Jim went on to play college baseball at the University of Michigan. There, he continued to shine. In 1987, he won the Golden Spikes Award, given to the best amateur baseball player in the country. That honor helped launch him into the major leagues when the California Angels selected him in the first round of the 1988 MLB draft.

Unlike most players, Jim skipped the minor leagues entirely. He went straight from college to the majors, making his debut in 1989. That season, he finished with a 12-12 record and a solid 3.92 ERA— impressive numbers for any rookie, let alone one with the kind of challenge he faced. Over the next 10 years, he played for several teams, including the Angels, New York Yankees, Chicago White Sox, and Milwaukee Brewers.

The Unforgettable No-Hitter

On September 4, 1993, Jim Abbott made history while pitching for the Yankees. He threw a **no-hitter** against the Cleveland Indians—one of baseball's most significant accomplishments. That day, Jim showed the world what he was truly capable of. With focus, confidence, and skill, he controlled the game from start to finish. For many fans, it was a moment they'd never forget; for Jim, it was the highlight of a career built on determination.

The Mindset of a Winner

Jim Abbott's success wasn't just about his physical ability but his **mindset**. He never let his condition define him. Instead, he found ways to turn it into a strength.

Creative Thinking

Jim had to be creative from the beginning. The way he learned to pitch and field with one hand was something he developed through experimentation, practice, and sheer determination. But his creativity didn't stop with his glove. On the mound, he was a thinker. He studied hitters, learned their weaknesses, and adjusted his approach accordingly. His brain was just as powerful as his arm.

Determination

Jim had to prove himself again and again. There were always people saying he couldn't make it. But instead of getting discouraged, he used those doubts to fuel his fire. He worked harder, trained smarter, and stayed focused on his goals. He didn't want special treatment—he wanted to be judged like any other player.

As Jim once said, "I wanted to prove I could pitch, not that I could pitch with one hand."

Positive Attitude

Perhaps most importantly, Jim Abbott always chose to stay positive. He focused on what he could do, not what he couldn't. That mindset helped him overcome obstacles and gave hope to others facing challenges.

He often spoke to fans about the power of embracing difficulties. He says, "Sometimes adversity is what you need to face to become successful." His story became a source of strength for people everywhere, especially kids who needed a role model.

A Lasting Legacy

Even after retiring from baseball, Jim didn't stop inspiring people. He became a speaker and author, sharing his life experiences with audiences worldwide. In his book, *Imperfect: An Improbable Life*, he talks honestly about the ups and downs of his journey and reminds readers of the importance of resilience.

Jim's impact goes far beyond sports. For people with disabilities, he's a shining example of what's possible. His story reminds us that no challenge is too big if we meet it with courage, creativity, and heart.

What Teens Can Learn from Jim Abbott

Jim Abbott's life is filled with lessons that can help any young person face tough times and dream big:

1. **Think Creatively** – There's always more than one way to reach your goal. Don't be afraid to try something new.

2. **Adapt and Keep Going** – Life doesn't always go as planned, but adapting and pushing forward makes you stronger.

3. **Work Hard and Stay Determined** – Believing in yourself and putting in the effort can silence doubters.

4. **Stay Positive** – Focus on what you can do instead of what you can't. A good attitude opens doors.

5. **Be an Inspiration** – When you overcome something challenging, your story can give others hope.

Jim Abbott's journey proves that greatness isn't about being perfect—it's about refusing to give up. His grit, creativity, and unwavering positivity showed the world what's possible. His message to young people is clear: no matter your challenges, you have the power to rise, inspire others, and chase your dreams.

MUHAMMAD ALI

The Champion Who Fought
For His Beliefs

The world remembers Cassius Marcellus Clay Jr.—better known as Muhammad Ali—not just for his legendary boxing skills, but for his unwavering courage in standing up for his beliefs. With dazzling talent and bold conviction, Ali became a global icon. From winning Olympic gold to being banned from boxing for refusing to fight in the Vietnam War, Ali showed the world what it means to be fearless, both in the ring and in life.

From Louisville to the Limelight

Muhammad Ali was born in January 1942, in Louisville, Kentucky, during a time of segregation and profound racial injustice in the United States. Growing up in a working-class neighborhood, Ali experienced discrimination firsthand. These early experiences shaped his desire to succeed and fueled his fire.

At age 12, Ali's journey into boxing began after someone stole his bicycle. Angry and determined to confront the thief, he met Joe Martin, a local police officer and boxing coach, who encouraged him to train instead. That moment sparked a passion to change Ali's life—and the world.

As an amateur, Ali stood out for his speed, flair, and charm. At just 18, he won a gold medal at the 1960 Rome Olympics. Soon after, he turned professional and quickly made headlines for his talent and personality. In 1964, he shocked the world by defeating Sonny Liston to become the world's heavyweight champion. He proudly declared, "I am the greatest!"—a phrase that would follow him forever.

A Bold Stand: Refusing the Vietnam War

In 1967, at the height of his boxing career, Ali made a decision that would change everything. He refused to serve when drafted into the U.S. Army during the Vietnam War.

Ali was a member of the Nation of Islam and stood by his religious and moral beliefs. "I ain't got no quarrel with them Viet Cong," he famously said. To him, fighting in the war meant supporting a system that continued to oppress Black Americans at home. He believed it was wrong to be forced to fight people abroad when there was still injustice in his own country.

That decision came at a high price. Ali was stripped of his title, banned from boxing for nearly four years, and faced the risk of jail time. Public opinion was divided—some called him a hero, others called him unpatriotic. But through it all, Ali stood his ground. He would not betray his beliefs for the sake of fame or fortune.

A Fighter in and out of the Ring

Ali's strength wasn't just physical, but also mental, emotional, and deeply rooted in his values.

Unshakable Confidence

Ali was known for his confidence. He called himself "The Greatest," then backed it up with incredible performances in the ring. He believed in himself with everything he had, which helped him overcome fear, pressure, and the most formidable opponents.

One of the most outstanding examples was the 1974 **"Rumble in the Jungle"** match against George Foreman. Using his clever "rope-a-dope" strategy, Ali let Foreman tire himself out, then took control and won by knockout in the eighth round. It wasn't just a boxing win but a masterclass in mental toughness, patience, and self-trust.

Sticking to His Principles

Even when it cost him everything, Ali refused to back down from what he believed. When asked if he regretted his stance on the war, he didn't hesitate. He said, "I have nothing to lose by standing up for my beliefs." His religion, dignity, and love for his people meant more to him than championships.

Because of this, Ali became more than a sports star—a symbol of resistance and a voice for civil rights. His bravery inspired others to speak up and fight back against injustice.

Comeback and Resilience

When Ali was finally allowed to return to boxing in 1970, many doubted he could still perform at the highest level. But he proved them wrong again. He reclaimed the heavyweight championship twice, in 1974 and 1978, solidifying his legacy as one of the greatest boxers ever.

Even in his most challenging moments—whether facing Joe Frazier in brutal battles or enduring the physical toll of his sport—Ali never gave in. His resilience made him a legend.

Strength Beyond Words

Ali didn't just fight with his fists; he also used his words. He was quick-witted, poetic, and fearless in trash talk. But behind the rhymes and bold lines was a strategy: to get inside his opponent's head. His mind was just as powerful as his punch.

In the ring, he withstood pain and pressure like few others could. His ability to keep going, even when the odds were against him, was one of his greatest strengths.

More Than a Boxer

Muhammad Ali's legacy extends far beyond the boxing world. In his later years, he focused on humanitarian work—fighting poverty, promoting peace, and helping others. Though Parkinson's disease slowed his body, his spirit never faded. His courage, humility, and love for everyone inspired millions.

Ali paved the way for athletes to use their platforms for more than entertainment. Today, his influence can be seen in stars like Colin Kaepernick, LeBron James, and many others who speak out for social justice. He made it okay—and powerful—for athletes to take a stand.

Lessons for Teens

Muhammad Ali's life is full of lessons that can help young people build strength, purpose, and courage:

1. **Believe in Yourself** – Confidence starts from within. Trust your abilities, even when others don't.

2. **Stand Up for What's Right** – Don't be afraid to defend your values, even when it's hard.

3. **Keep Going** – Challenges will come, but you can overcome them with effort and determination.

4. **Use Your Voice** – Your voice matters. Speak up when something is wrong. You can make a difference.

5. **Be Brave in the Face of Struggle** – True greatness comes from how you respond to hardship.

Ali's Enduring Message

Muhammad Ali showed the world that real strength is not just in muscles or medals—it's in your heart, beliefs, and actions. From Louisville to the world stage, he stood tall through every fight, inside and outside the ring.

Ali's life reminds us that true greatness comes from standing for what's right, believing in yourself, and using your influence to help others. Ali's message is clear for any young person facing obstacles: **Be bold. Be strong. And never be afraid to fight for what matters.**

SIMONE BILES

Courage, Focus, and Redefining Success

Simone Biles is one of the greatest gymnasts the world has ever seen. With 32 Olympic and World Championship medals, she has set records and stunned audiences with her power, skill, and creativity. But what truly makes her a hero isn't just her flips and gold medals—her courage, honesty, and determination to care for herself, even when the world was watching.

Simone's story is not just about winning medals. It's about growing through tough times, standing up for what matters, and showing the world that real strength comes from within.

A Tough Start

Simone Biles was born in Columbus, Ohio, on March 14, 1997. Her early life wasn't easy. Her mother struggled with addiction, and Simone, along with her siblings, was placed in foster care at a young age. Moving from home to home, she experienced fear and uncertainty.

When Simone was six, her grandparents, Ron and Nellie Biles, adopted her and her younger sister, Adria. They gave the girls a safe, loving home where they could finally grow and thrive. One day during a daycare field trip, Simone tried gymnastics—and immediately stood out. The coaches noticed her natural talent, and soon, she was enrolled in regular classes. Gymnastics became her safe place, where she could express herself and shine.

Even though she now had a stable home, Simone still carried emotional scars from her early years. But those tough times helped shape her strength instead of holding her back. "My journey wasn't easy," she once said, "but I wouldn't change a thing. It gave me the strength and grit to become who I am today."

A Star Is Born

By the time Simone was 14, she had decided to go all in on gymnastics. She trained hard—sometimes more than 30 hours a week—pushing herself to improve daily. Her coaches were amazed by her focus, work ethic, and talent.

In 2013 Simone exploded onto the international scene by winning the all-around title at the World Championships. She didn't just win—she dominated. Over the next few years, she kept making history, becoming the first woman to win five all-around World Championship titles and introducing new moves so difficult they were named after her.

Simone amazed the world with her power, precision, and grace. But behind every gold medal was a young woman working incredibly hard and focused on her goals.

Putting Mental Health First

In 2021, something surprising happened. During the Tokyo Olympics, Simone withdrew from several events. She explained that she was experiencing the "twisties"—a mental block that made her lose her sense of direction midair. That made competing dangerous, both physically and emotionally.

Many people supported her. Some didn't understand. But Simone stood firm. She explained, "We also have to focus on ourselves. Because at the end of the day, we're human, too."

By stepping back, Simone sent a powerful message: mental health matters just as much as physical health. Her choice helped athletes worldwide realize it's okay to care for your mind and ask for help when needed. She showed bravery, which doesn't always mean pushing through pain—it sometimes means knowing when to stop and heal.

The Champion's Mindset

Simone Biles's greatness comes not just from her physical skills but from her strong and steady mindset.

Courage to Speak Up

When Simone made the tough decision to step away from the competition in Tokyo, she broke a huge barrier. Athletes are often expected to keep going no matter what, even when it's not safe. Simone changed that. She proved that true strength is knowing your limits and caring for yourself, even when it's hard.

She also used her voice to advocate for others. Simone was one of the athletes who spoke out about being abused by former USA Gymnastics doctor Larry Nassar. She demanded justice and change, helping make the sport safer for future generations. Her bravery helped others feel less alone.

Laser-Sharp Focus

Simone's focus has always been one of her superpowers. She stays locked in, whether in front of thousands of fans or practicing quietly in the gym. That focus helped her land nearly impossible moves with incredible control.

Even off the mat, her focus shines. She's stayed committed to improving gymnastics and making it safer and more supportive. She doesn't just perform—she leads.

Discipline and Dedication

From the moment she started gymnastics, Simone was all in. Her discipline and work ethic have been key to her success. She trains hard, sets high standards, and always works to improve—even after reaching the top.

After the Tokyo Olympics, Simone returned to competition. She brought the same fire, commitment, and love for the sport she always had. That comeback wasn't about winning more medals but honoring her passion and showing resilience.

Her Lasting Impact

Simone Biles is more than a gymnast—she's a role model, a mental health advocate, and a game-changer. Her bravery in speaking out about mental health, her honesty about her struggles, and her continued excellence in gymnastics have inspired people of all ages.

She's helped create a new definition of what it means to be a champion. It's not just about medals. It's about staying true to yourself, caring for your well-being, and using your voice to help others.

Future gymnasts—and young people everywhere—can look to Simone as proof that it's okay to be human, vulnerable, and take time to heal.

Lessons for Teens

Simone Biles's journey is full of important lessons for young people trying to face their challenges:

1. **Take Care of Your Mental Health** – Your mind is as essential as your body. Ask for help, take breaks, and don't fear putting yourself first.

2. **Stay Focused** – Keep your eyes on your goals. Block out distractions and give your best effort, one step at a time.

3. **Be Brave** – It takes courage to speak up, especially when others don't understand. Stand firm in your truth.

4. **Practice Discipline** – Success doesn't happen overnight. Hard work, consistency, and practice lead to real progress.

5. **Use Your Voice for Good** – You can make a difference. Whether it's in your school, community, or team, speak up and support what's right.

Redefining What It Means to Win

Simone Biles showed the world that success isn't only about medals or records. It's about honoring who you are, facing life's challenges with bravery, and using your journey to uplift others. From foster care to the top of the Olympic podium—and back again—her story proves that strength comes in many forms.

For every teen who's ever felt unsure, overwhelmed, or pressured, Simone's message is simple but powerful: You are more than your achievements. You are worthy of care, rest, and kindness—especially from yourself.

USAIN BOLT

Sprinting Beyond Limits

U sain Bolt, often called the "Fastest Man Alive," changed the track and field world forever. With eight Olympic gold medals and world records in the 100-meter and 200-meter sprints, he became a global superstar—not just for his speed, but for his joyful spirit and larger-than-life personality.

But Bolt's journey wasn't always smooth. He faced serious challenges along the way, including health problems and doubts about whether he could succeed in sprinting: his confidence, love for what he did, and refusal to give up set him apart.

Growing Up Fast

Usain St. Leo Bolt was born on August 21, 1986, in the small town of Sherwood Content in Jamaica. As a kid, he was energetic and loved playing cricket and soccer. Coaches soon noticed that his real gift was speed—he could run faster than almost anyone his age.

By age 15, Bolt was already winning on the world stage. In 2002, he became the youngest-ever gold medalist at the World Junior Championships. But even with early success, things weren't easy.

Bolt had scoliosis, which caused his spine to curve, making one leg slightly longer. It led to frequent injuries, especially in his hamstrings, and raised serious concerns about his future as a sprinter. Some people even said he was too tall—at 6'5", he didn't look like the typical compact, powerful sprinter.

But Bolt wasn't about to let those things stop him.

Turning Challenges into Strengths

Instead of giving up, Bolt worked with his coaches and doctors to manage his scoliosis. He followed a special training plan, including core exercises, flexibility drills, and physical therapy. Over time, his condition improved, and he learned to use his height and long legs to his advantage.

Bolt's powerful stride became part of what made him unstoppable. He didn't just accept his differences—he used them to rewrite the rules of sprinting.

The Mindset of a Champion

What truly set Bolt apart wasn't just his body—it was his mindset. He believed in himself, loved what he did, and was never afraid to work hard to improve.

Confidence on the Track

Usain Bolt had confidence like no one else. Whether it was before a big race or during a press conference, he always showed belief in his abilities. Even when others doubted him, Bolt stayed sure of himself, and that self-belief gave him strength.

At the 2008 Beijing Olympics, Bolt amazed the world by running 9.69 seconds in the 100 meters, even slowing down to celebrate before the finish line. That moment showed the world his speed, yes—but also his courage and coolness under pressure.

Bolt kept that confidence through highs and lows. When he got injured or lost a race, he didn't give up. He used those moments to grow and come back stronger.

Joy in Competition

One thing fans loved about Bolt was how much fun he had. Before races, he would smile, dance, and strike his signature lightning bolt pose. He joked with reporters and waved to the crowd. He reminded everyone that sports are supposed to be exciting and joyful.

But Bolt's playfulness wasn't just for show. By staying relaxed and happy, he kept pressure from getting to him. That helped him perform better, even when the stakes were high.

His joy was contagious—he brought energy to every race and helped make track and field more popular worldwide.

Hard Work Behind the Scenes

Bolt's natural talent was impressive, but his work ethic made him great. Behind the cameras and the fun, he trained hard every day. He followed strict routines focused on power, speed, and perfecting every part of his race, from start to finish.

He also studied his races to find small ways to improve. Bolt never stopped learning and pushing himself, whether getting faster out of the blocks or fine-tuning his stride. His dedication paid off in a big way.

At the 2009 World Championships in Berlin, Bolt ran the 100 meters in 9.58 seconds and the 200 meters in 19.19 seconds—both world records still stand today. Those jaw-dropping performances came from years of hard work, innovative training, and a never-quit attitude.

A Legacy That Lives On

Usain Bolt's legacy goes far beyond medals and records. He made sprinting exciting and fun to watch. His smile, confidence, and electrifying performances brought new fans to the sport and inspired a new generation of athletes.

Off the track, Bolt gives back through the Usain Bolt Foundation, which supports education and sports programs, especially in Jamaica.

He wants to help young people believe in themselves and reach their dreams, just like he did.

Lessons for Teens

Usain Bolt's life teaches powerful lessons for any young person who wants to overcome challenges and achieve something remarkable:

1. **Believe in Yourself** – Confidence is key. Trust your abilities, even when others doubt you.

2. **Find Joy in What You Do** – Loving your work helps you push through tough times and enjoy the journey.

3. **Turn Challenges into Strengths** – Instead of giving up, adapt. Use your differences to your advantage.

4. **Work Hard Every Day** – Success takes more than talent. It takes discipline, dedication, and effort.

5. **Inspire Others** – Your journey can lift others. Share your story and lead with kindness and positivity.

Sprinting Toward Greatness

Usain Bolt didn't let scoliosis, injuries, or doubts hold him back. He turned his challenges into fuel and showed the world how to sprint with joy, power, and heart. He became a legend—not just because he was fast, but because he believed in himself and loved what he did.

For any teen who's ever faced setbacks, Bolt's story reminds that greatness isn't about being perfect—it's about rising above, one step at a time.

He developed into the best sprinter ever by showing confidence and joy, propelling his relentless work. Through his life story, Bolt teaches young people that exceptional achievement results from a mindset combined with resilience to surpass their limitations.

BETHANY HAMILTON

Courage Beyond the Waves

T he world knows Bethany Hamilton as a person who embodies extreme determination and resilience. From a young rising star in surfing to an international inspiration, her journey proves that even life's most challenging moments can become the start of something extraordinary. When Bethany lost her left arm in a shark attack at just 13 years old, she didn't let the tragedy stop her. Instead, she turned her pain into power, showing that courage and gratitude can lead to greatness.

Early Life and Passion for Surfing

Bethany Meilani Hamilton was born in Lihue, Hawaii, on February 8, 1990. Surrounded by waves and sunshine, surfing became more than a hobby—it was a way of life. Her parents, Tom and Cheri Hamilton, were surfers, and Bethany began riding waves when she was five. By age eight, she competed in local contests and quickly stood out for her talent and fearless spirit.

Bethany knew from early on that she wanted to be a professional surfer. Living in Kauai, where the ocean was always nearby, she found peace and purpose in the water. Her hard work paid off with sponsorship deals; by age 13, she was well on her way to a promising career.

But everything changed one calm October morning in 2003.

The Shark Attack: A Life-Altering Moment

On October 31, 2003, Bethany surfed with friends at Tunnels Beach. The ocean was peaceful, and the conditions were perfect. While lying on her board, her left arm hanging in the water, a 14-foot tiger shark attacked. In an instant, she lost her arm.

Bethany's friends acted fast, using her surfboard leash as a tourniquet to slow the bleeding and helping her paddle to shore. She had lost over half her blood, yet she remained calm and trusted in her faith. Her survival was nothing short of a miracle, made possible by the quick actions of her friends and her deep belief in God.

The recovery ahead was challenging. Bethany had to relearn how to live and surf with only one arm. For most people, that might have been the end of their dreams. But for Bethany, it was just the beginning of an incredible comeback.

The Winning Mindset

Bethany's return to surfing and competition didn't happen by luck. It was fueled by a mindset built on courage, gratitude, and refusing to let challenges define her.

Courage in the Face of Adversity

Just one month after the attack, Bethany was back in the water. That decision took tremendous courage. She faced her fears head-on, refusing to let them control her future. She once said, "I don't need easy; I just need possible," a simple but powerful statement about her outlook on life.

Bethany didn't just get back on the board—she competed at the highest level. She developed new techniques to adapt to surfing with one arm. She learned how to duck dive, stabilize the board, and maneuver through waves using only one arm and stronger leg work. These changes didn't limit her—they showed her creativity and drive to overcome.

Gratitude Amidst Challenges

One of the most inspiring things about Bethany is her deep sense of gratitude. Instead of focusing on what she lost, she focused on what she still had—her family, her faith, her passion, and her future. Her positive attitude helped her move forward and find joy, even through the pain.

Bethany credits much of her strength to her relationship with God. She believes her survival and recovery had a purpose: to inspire others. Rather than asking "Why me?" she asked, "How can I use this to help someone else?" That shift in perspective gave her power and peace.

Refusing to Be Defined by Limitations

Bethany's actions speak louder than words. In 2004, just one year after the attack, she won her first national title at the NSSA National Championships. She continued to compete against top athletes with two arms, showing that hard work and determination could overcome any physical challenge.

In 2007, Bethany's story was shared through her autobiography, Soul Surfer, which later became a major movie. Her journey reminded everyone that true greatness comes not from being perfect but rising after we fall.

Legacy and Impact

Bethany's influence reaches far beyond the world of surfing. Through her work with the Friends of Bethany Foundation, she supports amputees and trauma survivors, offering hope and practical help. Her story inspires young athletes, faith communities, and people facing various difficulties.

Bethany's life is a powerful example of how creativity and adaptation can help us overcome life's limits. She found new ways to do what she loved, and in doing so, showed others how to find strength in their challenges.

Lessons for Teens

Bethany Hamilton's journey is filled with lessons that can help young people face their obstacles with courage and hope:

1. **Face Fear Head-On** – Courage isn't about never being afraid. It's about taking action even when you are.

2. **Practice Gratitude** – Focusing on what you have, rather than what you've lost, helps build strength and resilience.

3. **Adapt and Innovate** – When life changes your path, find new ways forward. Be creative and stay open to learning.

4. **Refuse to Be Defined by Limitations** – Your circumstances don't limit your potential. Your mindset shapes it.

5. **Find Purpose in Adversity** – Your most challenging moments can become the reasons you inspire others. Let your struggles give you strength.

Riding Life's Waves

Bethany Hamilton's story teaches us that we can turn pain into purpose and setbacks into comebacks. Her shark attack could have ended her surfing career, but she refused to give up. Through her faith, determination, and creative spirit, she returned to the sport she loved and built a legacy of hope.

Bethany's message is clear for every young person facing something difficult: You are stronger than your obstacles. Keep going, keep growing, and never let fear decide your future. Like Bethany, you can ride the waves of life with courage and purpose.

LEBRON JAMES

Vision, Hard Work, and Empowering Others

LeBron James is not just one of the greatest basketball players of all time—he's also a leader, a role model, and a voice for change. He has proven himself on the court with four NBA championships, two Olympic gold medals, and countless awards. But LeBron's story is much bigger than basketball. He rose from a tough childhood to become a global icon, using his success to help others. His journey shows what can happen when you combine vision, dedication, and a desire to lift others.

Early Life and Challenges

LeBron Raymone James was born in Akron, Ohio, on December 30, 1984. He was raised by his mother, Gloria James, who was just 16 years old when he was born. Life was difficult for them. They moved often, staying with friends or family, and faced financial struggles that made it hard for LeBron to stay stable or focused on school.

Despite these challenges, LeBron had a natural gift for sports. When he was nine, a local football coach named Frank Walker introduced him to organized basketball. That small step changed everything. LeBron fell in love with the game, and it quickly became his escape and his focus.

Even as a kid, he worked hard to get better. By the time he entered high school at St. Vincent–St. Mary, LeBron was already a basketball star. But the pressure to succeed and the realities of growing up without much could have pushed him off course. Instead, he used those challenges to drive himself forward.

Rising to Stardom

LeBron's high school years were nothing short of amazing. He led his team to three state championships and was named one of the top high school players in the country. His talent was so remarkable that he appeared on the cover of Sports Illustrated as a junior with the headline "The Chosen One."

In 2003, straight out of high school, LeBron entered the NBA Draft and was selected by the Cleveland Cavaliers as the number one overall pick. From that moment, the pressure was on—but he delivered. Over the years, he became one of the most dominant players in the league, winning championships, MVP awards, and the respect of fans worldwide.

The Winning Mindset

LeBron James's greatness comes from more than just physical talent. His mindset—focused on vision, hard work, and helping others—has been the proper foundation of his success.

Vision

LeBron always had a clear idea of where he wanted to go. Even as a teenager, he saw basketball as a way to change not just his own life, but the lives of those around him. Big-picture thinking helped him stay focused, make wise choices, and remain strong under pressure.

As he got older, LeBron expanded that vision beyond sports. He co-founded SpringHill Entertainment, a company that creates movies and shows with powerful messages. He also launched Uninterrupted, a digital platform where athletes can share their stories and speak honestly. Through these efforts, he has helped reshape how athletes are seen, not just as performers, but as people with voices that matter.

Hard Work

LeBron is famous for his dedication to training. He takes care of his body and mind with the same intensity he brings to the game. He studies plays, watches films, and practices constantly. Even as he's gotten older, he continues to adapt and stay at the top of his game.

Off the court, LeBron works just as hard. Whether it's building businesses, mentoring young athletes, or creating community programs, he puts in the effort. His journey proves that talent alone isn't enough—success comes from constant effort and a strong work ethic.

Lifting Others

What truly sets LeBron apart is how much he cares about giving back. He has used his success to support others, especially kids from tough backgrounds like his own. In 2018, he opened the I PROMISE School in Akron, a public school created to help at-risk children and their families. The school offers free tuition, meals, transportation, and guaranteed college scholarships for graduates.

He has invested millions of dollars into education, housing, and community programs through the LeBron James Family Foundation. He once said, "I'm not just a basketball player. I want to be a change agent." And he has lived up to that promise.

Legacy and Impact

LeBron's legacy goes far beyond basketball. He has shown that athletes can be leaders, entrepreneurs, and changemakers. He has discussed important issues like racial justice, voting rights, and education. His willingness to use his voice and take action has earned him respect far beyond the court.

He has also changed the way young athletes think about success. For LeBron, success isn't just about winning games—it's about making life better for others. That mindset has inspired millions worldwide to dream bigger and work harder.

Lessons for Teens

LeBron James's journey is full of powerful lessons for young people trying to overcome obstacles and reach their goals:

1. **Have a Vision** – Know where you want to go and stay focused on it, even when things get tough.

2. **Work Hard** – Success doesn't come easy. It takes effort, discipline, and a willingness to grow.

3. **Lift Others**– Use your skills and success to help and make a difference.

4. **Stay Resilient** – Don't let setbacks stop you. Keep pushing forward and learn from every challenge.

5. **Be a Leader** – Lead by example and use your actions to inspire and guide the people around you.

A Life Bigger Than Basketball

LeBron James's story is about more than sports. It's about rising from hardship, staying focused, and using your gifts to help others. He didn't let his past hold him back. Instead, he worked hard, believed in his dream, and built a life full of purpose.

For teens facing challenges, LeBron's message is powerful: no matter where you start, you can build a life that lifts others and leaves a lasting impact. It's not just about being the best—it's about making the world better along the way.

MICHAEL JORDAN

The Relentless Pursuit of Greatness

ichael Jordan, widely known as the greatest basketball player of all time, didn't begin his journey as a guaranteed star. His rise to greatness is a story of determination, resilience, and belief in hard work. Before he earned six NBA championships and became the face of global basketball, Jordan faced a moment that could have ended it all: being cut from his high school basketball team. For many, that might have been a stopping point. For Jordan, it was the beginning of something extraordinary.

The Early Years

Michael Jeffrey Jordan was born on February 17, 1963, in Brooklyn, New York, and raised in Wilmington, North Carolina. He was the fourth of five children in a close-knit family. His parents, James and Deloris Jordan, taught him the value of discipline, effort, and responsibility. From a young age, Michael was competitive, whether playing sports with his siblings or working hard in the classroom. His father once said, "What he puts his mind to, he'll achieve."

Interestingly, basketball wasn't his first love. Jordan showed promise in baseball and even football before falling in love with basketball. But his road to success wasn't smooth. As a high school sophomore, standing at only 5'10", he was considered too short and not physically ready for varsity basketball. Despite his potential, he was cut from the team at Laney High School. It was heartbreaking, but it would become one of his life's most crucial turning points.

The Turning Point: Rejection as Motivation

He was devastated when Jordan learned he didn't make the varsity team. He cried alone at home, crushed by the disappointment. But instead of giving up, he promised himself that he would never feel that kind of disappointment again.

He poured himself into practice, spending hours each day shooting baskets in his driveway, running drills, and sharpening every part of his game. He joined the junior varsity team and dominated the court, scoring big and gaining attention. By the following year, he had grown taller, stronger, and more skilled and made the varsity team.

That experience taught him to use rejection as motivation. Looking back, Jordan said, "It was probably the best thing that ever happened to me because it made me know what disappointment felt like. And I knew I didn't want to have that feeling again."

The Winning Mindset

Jordan's strength wasn't just in his athletic skills—it was in his mindset. His refusal to be outworked and his ability to stay mentally tough in every situation separated him from others.

Relentless Practice

Jordan became famous for his work ethic. He was usually the first to arrive at the gym and the last to leave. Every practice was a chance to improve. Dean Smith, his college coach at the University of North Carolina, once said, "Michael's greatest strength is that he is always willing to work harder than anyone else."

In the NBA, his reputation grew. He trained hard, studied his opponents, and worked tirelessly to master every move. Jordan perfected the minor details, whether a simple layup or a game-winning fadeaway shot. His approach was simple: the game becomes easier if you push yourself harder in practice.

Turning Failure into Fuel

Failure never stopped Michael Jordan—it fueled him. He missed thousands of shots and lost hundreds of games throughout his career. But he used every failure as a lesson.

One of his most famous quotes explains it best: "I've missed more than 9,000 shots in my career. I've lost almost 300 games. I've been trusted to take the game-winning shot and missed twenty-six times. I've failed over and over and over again in my life. And that is why I succeed."

Jordan saw failure as part of the path to success. He didn't fear mistakes—instead, he learned from them and returned stronger.

Mental Toughness and Focus

Jordan was known for staying focused in the most challenging situations. He never let distractions shake him, whether playing in front of loud crowds or during critical moments. His ability to remain calm and collected earned him the nickname "His Airness."

One of the most outstanding examples of his mental strength was during the 1997 NBA Finals—now called the "Flu Game." Despite being sick with flu-like symptoms, Jordan scored 38 points, leading the Chicago Bulls to victory. His performance became a symbol of courage, grit, and heart.

Unwavering Confidence

Jordan's confidence was built on preparation and belief. He trusted himself because he knew how much work he had put in. Even when others doubted him, he never doubted himself.

His confidence wasn't about showing off but knowing he was ready. He embraced pressure and delivered when it mattered most.

Legacy of Greatness

Michael Jordan's journey from a rejected high school player to a six-time NBA champion is one of the most inspiring stories in sports. He earned five MVP awards, 10 scoring titles, and became a worldwide icon—but his true legacy is the message he left behind: anything is possible with hard work and perseverance.

Beyond basketball, Jordan became a cultural legend. His Air Jordan sneakers symbolized excellence, and his influence reached people of all ages and backgrounds. Despite his success, he remained focused on humility, discipline, and continuing to grow.

Lessons for Teens

Michael Jordan's life story is filled with valuable lessons that can help young people face their challenges:

1. **Turn Setbacks into Steppingstones** – Rejection isn't the end. It can be the beginning of something even greater.

2. **Work Harder Than Everyone Else** – Success comes to those who go the extra mile daily.

3. **Embrace Failure** – Every mistake is a chance to grow. Don't be afraid to try and fail.

4. **Stay Focused and Confident** – Believe in yourself and your abilities, even when things get tough.

5. **Be Resilient** – Push through challenges and never let obstacles define your future.

Chasing Greatness

Michael Jordan didn't become great overnight. He worked for it, sacrificed for it, and never gave up. His story shows that greatness isn't just about talent but passion, effort, and heart.

For teens facing struggles or setbacks, Jordan's story is a reminder that even the most challenging moments can lead to something incredible. With determination and the right mindset, you can rise above any challenge like he did.

CHLOE KIM

Flying High with Joy and Balance

C hloe Kim is a name people connect with snowboarding greatness. At just 17 years old, she won an Olympic gold medal and became the youngest woman to win in the halfpipe event. Her incredible performance launched her into international fame, but that success came with challenges. Chloe's path to the top taught her to stay strong mentally, keep a positive attitude, and understand the importance of stepping back to take care of herself.

Early Life and Path to Snowboarding Stardom

Chloe Kim was born on April 23, 2000, in Long Beach, California, to parents who had immigrated from South Korea. Her father, Jong Jin Kim, introduced her to snowboarding when she was only four. Even though he had no snowboarding experience, he completely supported Chloe's dreams. He often drove hours to the mountains so she could train.

Chloe quickly showed that she was a natural. By the time she was six, she was already entering competitions. Her fearless style and ability to land tough tricks made her stand out. She also had a fun, energetic personality that drew attention and made her a favorite in snowboarding.

At age 13, Chloe qualified for the 2014 Winter Olympics but was too young to compete. That didn't stop her from training harder. She continued perfecting her skills and even landed back-to-back 1080s, a trick few women could perform. By the time the 2018 Olympics in PyeongChang arrived, she was already a global star—and she lived up to the hype by winning gold.

The Pressure of Being a Prodigy

Chloe's fast rise to fame brought a lot of praise, but it also brought stress. While many saw her as a confident, fun-loving teen, Chloe was under immense pressure. Being in the spotlight and competing at such a high level affected her well-being.

"It was hard to have so many eyes on me at such a young age," Chloe said. "I felt like I had to be perfect all the time, and that pressure started to affect my mental health."

Training for competitions meant long hours on the mountain, intense physical demands, and nonstop travel. Even after winning Olympic gold, Chloe felt overwhelmed and exhausted. She was proud of her achievement, but also realized something important—she needed to care for herself just as much as she cared about winning.

The Winning Mindset

What sets Chloe Kim apart isn't just her talent on a snowboard—it's her mindset. She stays grounded with a joyful outlook, a playful spirit, and a strong focus on mental health.

A Positive Attitude

For Chloe, snowboarding isn't just about medals. It's about joy. She always reminds others to focus on having fun and enjoying the process instead of worrying about results. Snowboarding gives her a sense of freedom; she often describes the mountain as her happy place.

Instead of letting pressure control her, Chloe stays focused on what she loves most—being in the moment and doing what she enjoys. That positive mindset helps her handle both victories and setbacks with grace.

A Sense of Fun

Chloe's playful personality is part of why people love her so much. Whether laughing with teammates, sharing funny posts on social media, or showing off her unique tricks, she brings light and fun to everything she does.

But her fun-loving approach isn't just for show—it's part of her strategy. By keeping snowboarding enjoyable, she avoids burnout and stays motivated. Her focus on joy allows her to perform her best while reminding everyone that sports should be fun.

The Courage to Take Breaks

After her 2018 Olympic win, Chloe made a bold decision—she took a break from competition. She spent time on herself, started attending Princeton University, and explored other interests away from the spotlight.

Taking a break wasn't easy, but it was necessary. Chloe realized that she needed to reset and refocus. "I seized this moment to refresh my passion for snowboarding while regaining my love for the sport," she said.

By setting healthy boundaries and making time for her well-being, Chloe showed that athletes don't always need to push through. Sometimes, the bravest move is stepping back to take care of yourself.

Legacy and Impact

Chloe Kim's influence goes far beyond her gold medals. She has redefined what it means to be a champion, proving that success can include rest, fun, and staying true to yourself. She inspires people not just with her tricks, but with her honesty, her joy, and her advocacy for mental health.

As a first-generation Asian-American, Chloe uses her platform to speak up about diversity, representation, and inclusion in sports. She encourages young athletes of all backgrounds to believe in themselves and pursue their dreams.

Lessons for Teens

Chloe Kim's journey offers essential lessons for young people trying to succeed while staying grounded:

1. **Stay Positive** – Focus on the good, even during tough times. A positive mindset helps you move forward.

2. **Have Fun** – Find joy in what you do. Loving your work makes it easier to handle stress and challenges.

3. **Prioritize Mental Health** – Your well-being matters more than any achievement. Take care of yourself first.

4. **Set Boundaries** – It's okay to say no and take breaks. Doing what's best for you is always the right choice.

5. **Inspire Others** – Share what you've learned to help lift people around you.

Soaring with Balance

Chloe Kim shows that greatness doesn't have to come at the cost of joy. She's reached incredible heights through snowboarding while also staying down to earth. Her story teaches us that success isn't just about how high you go but how true you stay to yourself along the way.

Chloe's message for teens chasing big dreams is clear: stay joyful, stay balanced, and always remember to take care of yourself.

BILLIE JEAN KING

A Champion for Equality and Excellence

illie Jean King is known as a tennis legend and a fearless advocate for equality and justice. Her dedication to fair treatment in sports and society has made her a historic figure far beyond the court. Throughout her life, she fought against unfairness and worked hard to make women's tennis and sports in general a more level playing field. Billie Jean King changed the game in tennis and the world.

Early Life and Introduction to Tennis

Billie Jean Moffitt was born in Long Beach, California, on November 22, 1943. She grew up in a working-class family. Her father was a firefighter, and her mother was a homemaker. From a young age, Billie Jean loved playing sports. She often played softball and other games with neighborhood boys and always showed fierce determination.

Her life changed at age 11 when she picked up a tennis racket for the first time. Back then, tennis was considered a sport for wealthy people, and seeing kids from working-class families on the court wasn't common. But Billie Jean didn't let that stop her. She practiced on public courts using borrowed equipment and quickly showed she had a natural talent for the game.

As a teenager, she began competing in junior tournaments, earning recognition for her aggressive style and unshakable determination.

Rising to Stardom and Battling Sexism

Billie Jean made her mark on the international tennis scene in the early 1960s. In 1961, she won her first Wimbledon title in women's doubles. Over the next two decades, she won an incredible 39 Grand Slam titles, including 12 in singles.

But her journey wasn't easy. Throughout her career, Billie Jean faced constant sexism. Women's tennis players were often paid much less than men and didn't receive the same respect or recognition. Billie Jean knew that had to change. She realized early on that her platform as an athlete could help fight for fairness, and she made that her mission.

The Fight for Equal Pay

One of Billie Jean's biggest battles was equal pay for women in tennis. In 1970, upset by the massive pay gap between male and female players, she helped form the Virginia Slims Circuit—a group of nine women who broke away from the traditional tennis system to create a new path. Knowing it could hurt their careers, they took a risk, but they were determined to be treated fairly.

That bold move led to significant change. In 1973, Billie Jean helped create the Women's Tennis Association (WTA), giving female players their organization. That same year, the U.S. Open became the first Grand Slam tournament to offer equal prize money for men and women, largely thanks to Billie Jean's advocacy.

The "Battle of the Sexes"

One of Billie Jean's most famous moments came in 1973, when she faced off against Bobby Riggs in a tennis match known as the "Battle of the Sexes." Riggs, a former Wimbledon champion, claimed that women's tennis wasn't competitive, and that no woman could beat him, even at age 55.

Billie Jean saw the match as more than a game. She knew it was a chance to prove that women athletes deserved respect. On September 20, 1973, Billie Jean defeated Riggs in straight sets in front of over 30,000 fans and 90 million TV viewers.

The victory was about more than tennis. It was a powerful message that women could compete and succeed at the highest level. It inspired millions and helped change attitudes toward gender equality in sports and beyond.

The Winning Mindset

Billie Jean King's success came not just from talent, but from her mindset. She showed courage, discipline, and a deep belief in fairness and self-expression.

Fearlessness in Speaking Out

Billie Jean never stayed silent when something was wrong. She spoke out for women's rights, LGBTQ+ rights, and equal treatment in all areas of life. In 1981, she became one of the first major athletes to be openly gay, even though she knew it would cost her endorsements and support.

Despite the personal risks, she chose honesty over hiding. She believed in living truthfully and using her voice to make life better for others. Her bravery helped open doors for more acceptance and understanding in sports and society.

Tireless Advocacy

Even after her playing career ended, Billie Jean never stopped working for change. She founded the Women's Sports Foundation and the Billie Jean King Leadership Initiative to promote fairness and leadership in sports and workplaces.

She has inspired many athletes to use their voices for good, and her example shows that athletes can be influential leaders beyond the game.

Athletic Excellence

Billie Jean was a fierce competitor who worked hard every day to improve. She kept pushing herself to improve, even as she led major movements for equality. Her strong work ethic and passion for tennis helped her stay at the top of her game while fighting for justice.

She showed that it's possible to be both an elite athlete and a committed advocate, proving that dedication and heart can change the world.

Legacy and Impact

Billie Jean King's legacy stretches far beyond her 39 Grand Slam titles. She helped transform women's tennis, opened doors for future generations, and pushed society toward greater fairness and equality.

In 2009, President Obama awarded her the Presidential Medal of Freedom, the highest civilian honor in the United States. Today, she speaks out on equal pay, leadership, and inclusion issues.

She has inspired athletes, students, leaders, and everyday people who want to stand up for what's right.

Lessons for Teens

Billie Jean King's story teaches important lessons for young people who want to create positive change:

1. **Be Fearless** – Speak up for what's right, even when it's hard or unpopular.

2. **Advocate for Others** – Use your voice and position to help those who may not have the same opportunities.

3. **Strive for Excellence** – Work hard in your passion while staying committed to your values.

4. **Embrace Authenticity** – Be true to yourself and never hide your identity to please others.

5. **Keep Going** – Change takes time, and progress comes through steady effort and determination.

A Legacy of Courage

Billie Jean King's story is about more than winning titles—it's about standing up for fairness, breaking barriers, and making the world better. She showed the power of combining talent with purpose through every match she played and every cause she supported.

For teens who want to change the world, her message is simple: speak up, work hard, and never stop believing in the power of equality. Like Billie Jean King, you can be a champion in sports, in life, and the fight for a better future.

ERIC LEGRAND

Optimism and Living Life to the Fullest

E ric LeGrand was born on September 4, 1990, in Avenel, New Jersey. From an early age, he was known for his big personality, strong work ethic, and love for sports. Football quickly became his favorite, and his talent was shining bright by the time he was in high school at Colonia High.

2008, Eric earned a scholarship to play for the Rutgers University football team. He became a fan favorite for his powerful tackles and leadership on and off the field. By his junior year, he was seen as a future NFL player with big dreams and the drive to achieve them.

The Injury That Changed Everything

On October 16, 2010, during a kickoff play in a game against Army, Eric made a tackle that changed his life forever. He hit the opposing player head-on and immediately collapsed. The collision fractured his C3 and C4 vertebrae, leaving him paralyzed from the shoulders down.

Doctors told him he might never walk—or even breathe on his own—again. But Eric didn't let that stop his spirit. "I'm going to get through this," he told his family. "I'm going to fight." That moment began a new journey—one built on courage, optimism, and the will to inspire others.

The Winning Mindset

Since his injury, Eric LeGrand has lived with an unbreakable mindset filled with hope and purpose. He's become a powerful voice for strength, positivity, and living life with meaning.

Optimism in the Face of Adversity

From the start, Eric focused on what he could still do, not what he couldn't. Even though he couldn't move his body, his spirit stayed strong. He remained upbeat, talked with friends, laughed often, and chose gratitude daily.

Eric says he is thankful to be alive and believes every day brings a new chance to make an impact. That thinking has helped him get through therapy, hospital stays, and moments of uncertainty with grace and strength.

Determination to Inspire Others

Eric may have lost movement, but he found a new purpose. He began sharing his story through public speaking, TV interviews, and his book *Believe: My Faith and the Tackle That Changed My Life*. His message is simple but powerful: never give up, stay positive, and always seek your reason to keep going.

In 2013 Eric received the Jimmy V Award for Perseverance at the ESPYs. In his acceptance speech, he reminded everyone that perseverance isn't about having an easy road—it's about facing hard times with courage and continuing forward no matter what.

Living Life to the Fullest

Eric doesn't let his injury stop him from chasing joy and making a difference. He earned his degree from Rutgers University, started his foundation, and even opened a coffee shop—LeGrand Coffee House—in 2021. He says he wanted to create a space where people could gather, feel inspired, and build community.

He also works as a sports analyst, sharing his football knowledge with fans, and continues to stay involved with the Rutgers team. Every move he makes proves that he is still doing what he loves—just in a new way.

Legacy and Impact

Eric LeGrand's influence goes far beyond football. His strength has inspired people worldwide to face their challenges with courage. Through his foundation, Team LeGrand, he raises awareness about spinal cord injuries and funds research to help find a cure.

His story reminds people that life can still be full of joy, purpose, and love—even after something devastating. He has turned his toughest moment into a powerful mission to help others live better, dream bigger, and never stop believing in what's possible.

Lessons for Teens

Eric LeGrand's story offers important life lessons for young people facing challenging moments or looking for motivation:

1. **Stay Positive** – Focus on what you can do and keep a hopeful mindset even when things are hard.

2. **Find Purpose** – Let your struggles help you discover your reason to inspire and help others.

3. **Never Give Up** – Don't let setbacks define you. Keep pushing forward, no matter how tough things get.

4. **Embrace Gratitude** – Be thankful for what you have, even when life isn't perfect.

5. **Live Fully** – Chase your dreams and make every moment count. Life is worth living to the fullest.

A Symbol of Strength

Eric LeGrand shows us that muscles or trophies don't measure strength—it's measured by heart. His story proves you can face your biggest challenge and still rise, inspire, and shine. Eric has chosen to live with purpose, joy, and courage, from the football field to the hospital bed to the stage and beyond.

Eric's message is clear to teens who feel like giving up or facing something hard: what happens to you doesn't define you—how you respond does. Keep fighting, keep believing, and never stop living fully.

LIONEL MESSI

Rising Above Challenges to Redefine Greatness

L onel Messi is known worldwide as one of the greatest footballers in history. But his story is about more than trophies and goals—it's about rising above physical limitations, staying humble, and constantly striving to improve. Diagnosed with a growth hormone deficiency as a child, Messi didn't let that stop him. Instead, he used determination, focus, and quiet strength to rewrite what it means to be truly great.

Early Life and Diagnosis

Lionel Andrés Messi was born in Rosario, Argentina, on June 24, 1987. His talent was impossible to miss from when he was a small child. At age five, he was already dazzling fans with his skill while playing for a local club called Grandoli, coached by his father, Jorge.

Messi came from a working-class family where football was a way of life. But when he was 10, his future became uncertain. Doctors diagnosed him with a growth hormone deficiency (GHD), a condition that would stop him from growing normally without expensive daily treatments. The medicine cost around $900 a month—far more than his family could afford.

For many kids, such a diagnosis might have ended their dreams. But Messi refused to let go of his love for football. His determination only grew stronger.

Overcoming Growth Hormone Deficiency

Despite the challenge, Messi never lost his spark. Though shorter than most players, he stood out for his speed, vision, and control on the field. With the support of his family, they searched for ways to get him the care he needed.

In 2000, their prayers were answered. Scouts from FC Barcelona noticed Messi's rare talent. The club offered to pay for his treatment and invited him to join their famous youth academy, La Masia. At just 13 years old, Messi and his family moved to Spain, beginning a journey that would change football forever.

The Winning Mindset

Messi's success wasn't just about natural talent. His mindset—marked by humility, focus, and a relentless drive to improve—set him apart.

Humility

Even after becoming one of the most famous athletes in the world, Messi has stayed humble. He avoids the spotlight, focuses on his team, and lets his performance speak for itself. He treats teammates, fans, and even rivals with respect.

Messi often says that football is a team sport, and he always credits those around him for his achievements. His modesty and down-to-earth attitude have made him a beloved figure across the globe, not just for his skill but for his character.

Focus

From his early days at La Masia to breaking records with Barcelona and Argentina, Messi has remained intensely focused. He studies his opponents, trains hard, and works to improve every detail of his game.

He has faced many challenges—injuries, criticism, and pressure on the world stage—but never loses concentration. Whether a World Cup match or a league game, Messi brings the same calm focus and sharp decision-making that define true greatness.

Relentless Drive to Succeed

Messi's career is a testament to never settling. Even after winning every major football award, he continues to push himself. He trains daily, adapts his game, and looks for ways to improve his passing, shooting, and even his free kicks.

That same drive carried him through heartbreaks with the Argentine national team. After years of coming close, he finally led Argentina to win the Copa América in 2021. His emotional celebration showed how much it meant to him—and how years of hard work had paid off.

Legacy and Impact

Lionel Messi's legacy goes beyond football. His story proves that greatness isn't just about being the biggest or fastest heart, effort, and vision. He changed how people think about what it takes to be a champion.

Once seen as a weakness, his small stature became part of his greatness. He proved that imaginative play, skill, and discipline can beat size and strength. Messi's rise from a boy in Rosario to a global icon reminds us that true power comes from within.

Off the field, Messi has made a difference through his charitable work. He supports health care, education, and social programs for needy children through the Leo Messi Foundation. He uses his platform to make life better for others, reflecting the same kindness and humility that define his career.

Lessons for Teens

Lionel Messi's life offers powerful lessons for young people chasing dreams and facing challenges:

1. **Turn Challenges into Opportunities** – Let your obstacles push you to work harder and reach further.

2. **Stay Humble** – Kindness and respect will take you farther than ego ever could.

3. **Focus on Your Goals** – Tune out distractions and stay committed, no matter the pressure.

4. **Work Relentlessly** – Keep practicing, learning, and growing—even when success starts to come.

5. **Believe in Yourself** – Your mindset can overcome any limitation. Trust in your journey.

A Symbol of True Greatness

Lionel Messi's story is about more than winning. It's about holding onto your dreams, even when the odds are against you. It's about staying grounded while reaching the top. And it's about showing the world that greatness is built not just on talent, but on who you choose to be.

Messi's message is clear for teens facing hard times or big dreams: never let your limitations define you. Believe in yourself, stay humble, and work with everything you have. Like Messi, you can rise above and become something truly unforgettable.

NAOMI OSAKA

A Champion of Strength and Self-Care

Naomi Osaka rose to tennis stardom with stunning speed, becoming one of the sport's brightest stars. Osaka, known for her powerful serves, cool composure, and thoughtful personality, captured the world's attention for her victories and courage. While she reached the top of tennis, she also faced the heavy pressure that comes with fame. Instead of hiding her struggles, she chose honesty, putting her well-being first and becoming a symbol of strength, self-care, and change.

Early Life and Path to Tennis Stardom

Naomi Osaka was born on October 16, 1997, in Chūō-ku, Osaka, Japan. Her mother, Tamaki, is Japanese, and her father, Leonard François, is Haitian. Naomi grew up in a multicultural home with her older sister, Mari. Inspired by watching Venus and Serena Williams, their father began training both daughters in tennis, using the Williams sisters' success as a blueprint.

When Naomi was three, the family moved to the United States, eventually settling in Florida to give the girls better training opportunities. Even though money was tight, her parents were determined to support their daughters' dreams. They taught Naomi the importance of working hard, staying focused, and remaining humble.

In 2013, Naomi turned professional, and by 2018, she won her first Grand Slam title at the US Open, beating her idol, Serena Williams, in a highly publicized match. Osaka became a household name with that win and continued her rise with three more Grand Slam victories. But along with success came growing pressure and expectations.

The Challenge of Mental Health

As Naomi's popularity grew, so did the pressure to win and perform in the spotlight. The constant media attention and demands from fans and sponsors began to take a toll on her mental health. In 2021, Osaka made headlines when she withdrew from the French Open, choosing not to attend post-match press conferences for her mental well-being.

Her decision sparked global debate. Some criticized her, saying she avoided responsibility, while others praised her for bravely speaking out. In an essay for *Time* magazine, Osaka wrote, "It's OK not to be OK," encouraging others to talk openly about mental health.

By stepping away from the game and choosing therapy, rest, and joy, Osaka began redefining what it means to be a champion—not just in sports, but in life.

The Winning Mindset

Naomi Osaka's success comes not only from her tennis skills but from her mindset. She leads with honesty, resilience, and a strong belief in the importance of self-care.

Honesty

Osaka's willingness to talk about her struggles has made her a voice for athletes and young people everywhere. By sharing her emotional challenges, she has helped remove the stigma around mental health. Her honesty allows others to see that even champions face tough times—and that it's okay to ask for help.

She also practices self-awareness. Osaka pays attention to her emotions and knows when she needs time to rest and recharge. This ability to be honest with herself is a primary reason she's been able to take care of her mental well-being.

Resilience

Even when facing criticism or setbacks, Osaka continues to show strength. She doesn't give up. After taking time off, she returned to tennis with a renewed spirit. Each challenge has made her stronger, and she often talks about how obstacles help her grow.

During matches, she stays calm and focused. She's known for coming back from behind, saving match points, and playing with quiet determination.

Prioritizing Well-Being

Osaka is reshaping what success looks like in professional sports. Rather than pushing through at the cost of her health, she sets boundaries and puts herself first when needed. This bold choice has inspired athletes around the world to rethink how they care for their minds as well as their bodies.

Outside of tennis, Osaka enjoys spending time with her family, exploring her cultural roots, and expressing herself through fashion, art, and business. These moments of joy and balance help her stay centered and energized.

Legacy and Impact

Naomi Osaka's influence reaches far beyond tennis. By using her voice, she has sparked conversations about mental health, self-worth, and personal limits. She shows that strength isn't always about pushing through—it can also mean stepping back to take care of yourself.

She's also a strong advocate for social justice. At the 2020 US Open, she wore face masks with the names of Black victims of police violence, using her platform to raise awareness and honor their lives.

Through her actions, Osaka has shown that being a champion isn't just about winning—it's about standing up for what matters and encouraging others to do the same.

Lessons for Teens

Naomi Osaka's story offers powerful lessons for young people who want to find strength in their journey:

1. **Be Honest with Yourself** – It's okay not to feel OK. Listen to your emotions and speak up when you need support.

2. **Embrace Resilience** – Challenges can make you stronger. Keep growing through difficult moments.

3. **Prioritize Your Well-Being** – Taking care of your mental health is as important as chasing success.

4. **Set Boundaries** – It's okay to say no. Protect your peace and focus on what helps you feel whole.

5. **Use Your Voice** – Stand up for what you believe in. Your story can inspire change in the world.

True Strength Comes from Within

Naomi Osaka's journey shows that true greatness isn't just about trophies—it's about staying true to yourself, even when the world is watching. Her courage, honesty, and calm strength remind us that real power comes from within.

Osaka's story is a message of hope for teens navigating pressure, fear, or big dreams: you don't have to be perfect. You have to be you. And that is more than enough.

JESSE OWENS

Triumph in the Face of Adversity

J esse Owens is remembered as one of the greatest athletes in
history—not just for his incredible achievements on the track, but
for his dignity, courage, and strength in the face of injustice. His
story is one of triumph over racism, poverty, and pressure, and his
performance at the 1936 Berlin Olympics continues to inspire people
worldwide today.

Early Life and Challenges

James Cleveland Owens was born in Oakville, Alabama, on September 12, 1913, into a large sharecropping family. He was the youngest of ten children. When he was nine, his family moved to Cleveland, Ohio, for better opportunities. Life was still tricky, and Jesse helped support his family by working different jobs while attending school.

During his school years, Owens's athletic talent began to shine. His speed caught the attention of Charles Riley, a track coach at East Technical High School. Riley became his mentor, helping Jesse develop his running technique and pushing him to train hard. Owens quickly became a standout competitor, winning local and national track meets. Yet, even as his talent grew, so did the barriers. Owens faced racism at nearly every turn—separate facilities, limited opportunities, and constant discrimination. But instead of giving up, he used it as motivation to keep running forward.

The Road to the 1936 Olympics

Owens enrolled at Ohio State University, earning the nickname "Buckeye Bullet." He set multiple track records, and on May 25, 1935, he made sports history by breaking three world records and tying a fourth—all in just 45 minutes at the Big Ten Championships. It was a legendary performance.

Despite his success, Owens continued to face discrimination. While traveling for meetings, he was often denied access to hotels and restaurants. But he didn't let bitterness distract him. Instead, he kept his eyes on the 1936 Olympic Games in Berlin, Germany—an event that would test his athletic abilities and courage.

Adolf Hitler planned to use the Olympics to promote Nazi ideas about racial superiority. As a Black American athlete, Owens carried the heavy weight of challenging both racism at home and propaganda abroad.

The 1936 Berlin Olympics

Jesse Owens delivered one of the most powerful performances in Olympic history. He won four gold medals—in the 100 meters, 200 meters, long jump, and 4x100 meter relay. With each race, he shattered not just records, but also the racist beliefs being promoted in Berlin at the time.

One of the most memorable moments came during the long jump event. After two fouls, Owens was close to being disqualified. Then, in a surprising act of sportsmanship, German competitor Luz Long offered him advice. Owens followed it, made a clean jump, and eventually won gold while Long took silver. The two men shook hands and became friends, showing the world that respect could overcome politics and prejudice.

Back home, however, Owens returned to a country that still maltreated him. He wasn't invited to the White House, and racial segregation continued. Despite his global success, he was still seen as unequal in his country.

The Winning Mindset

What made Jesse Owens truly extraordinary was not just his talent—it was how he carried himself.

Grace Under Pressure

Owens remained calm and respectful even in the most stressful situations. Whether facing jeers from hostile crowds or discrimination in his daily life, he kept his focus. He didn't lash out. Instead, he let his actions speak.

During the long jump qualifying round, after two fouls, Owens had one last chance to advance. With the crowd watching and pressure building, he delivered a perfect jump. That moment defined his calm strength and focus under pressure.

Turning Adversity into Fuel

Owens used the racism he faced as motivation. Whenever someone doubted or maltreated him, his desire to prove them wrong was fueled. "The battles that count," he once said, "aren't the ones for gold medals. The struggles within yourself—that's where it's at."

For Owens, each race became more than a contest. It was an opportunity to show the world what strength, courage, and hard work could do.

Inspiring Through Dignity

Owens's quiet strength and respectful demeanor made him a role model for generations to come. He carried himself with grace, even when others didn't treat him with respect. He showed that determination and dignity could rise above hate and injustice.

Legacy and Impact

Jesse Owens changed history—not just with his athletic achievements, but with what he stood for. At a time when both Nazi Germany and the United States practiced racial discrimination, Owens's success challenged the idea that race determined worth or ability.

He received the Presidential Medal of Freedom in 1976, one of the highest civilian honors in the United States. The Jesse Owens Award honors his legacy and is given to the best track and field athletes each year. His story inspires athletes, students, and anyone facing complex challenges.

Lessons for Teens

Jesse Owens's life offers valuable lessons for teens striving to succeed and stand firm in the face of hardship:

1. **Stay Calm Under Pressure** – Don't let stress or negativity distract you. Stay focused on your goals.

2. **Use Challenges as Motivation** – Let your struggles make you stronger, not weaker.

3. **Inspire Through Actions** – Set an example for others by working hard and treating people with respect.

4. **Defy Limits** – Your abilities define you, not someone else's opinion. Push past what others expect.

5. **Practice True Sportsmanship** – Compete honorably and build bridges, even in harsh environments.

A Legacy That Runs Forever

Jesse Owens proved you can stand tall even when the world tries to hold you down. His victories at the 1936 Olympics were more than wins—they were acts of courage and hope. He showed that greatness doesn't come from gold medals alone, but from how you face the world.

For young people today, Jesse Owens remains a powerful reminder that no matter what obstacles you face, you can rise above and leave a lasting legacy with focus, dignity, and determination.

MICHAEL PHELPS

Mastering the Mind and Body

S wimming excellence represents the identity of Michael Phelps. With 28 Olympic medals—23 gold—he holds more than any athlete in history. But his success in the pool is only part of his story. Behind the records is a man who faced personal challenges, battled mental health struggles, and learned that true strength comes from knowing and caring for yourself, both physically and mentally.

Early Life and ADHD Diagnosis

Michael Fred Phelps II was born in Baltimore, Maryland, on June 30, 1985. He was the youngest of three siblings and grew up in a household where swimming was part of daily life. His older sisters, Whitney and Hilary, were competitive swimmers, and young Michael followed their lead.

At age seven, Michael was diagnosed with attention deficit hyperactivity disorder (ADHD). He had trouble sitting still in class, struggled to focus, and was often labeled a distraction. Teachers would get frustrated with him for fidgeting or tapping his pencil, and he frequently left class without finishing his work.

But in the water, Michael found peace. Swimming became an outlet for his boundless energy and a place to focus. It gave him structure and purpose. Bob Bowman's coach recognized his potential early and began shaping him into an elite athlete through a disciplined and demanding training program.

The Making of a Champion

Phelps's talent developed quickly. At just 15 years old, he qualified for the 2000 Sydney Olympics, becoming the youngest male swimmer to represent the U.S. in nearly 70 years. He didn't win a medal that year, but the experience sparked a hunger for success.

Over the next decade, Phelps dominated the sport. At the 2008 Beijing Olympics, he made history by winning eight gold medals, surpassing the previous record of seven. His powerful strokes, precise turns, and mental focus made him nearly unbeatable in the pool. Behind the scenes, he trained tirelessly—sometimes swimming six hours a day and covering up to 12 miles.

His rise to the top wasn't easy, but his work ethic and commitment made him a legend.

Struggles with Mental Health

Even as he stood on top of the podium, Phelps was battling struggles of a different kind. He felt lost after the 2012 London Olympics, where he won four golds and two silvers. Without a clear direction, he found himself slipping into depression.

He described those years as some of the darkest in his life. He felt alone and unsure of his purpose. His second DUI arrest in 2014 was a turning point. It forced him to face his struggles and finally ask for help.

Phelps entered a treatment center and began therapy. With the support of professionals, family, and friends, he started the process of healing. Speaking publicly about his experience, Phelps helped break the silence around mental health, especially among athletes. He showed that even champions can struggle—and that asking for help is a sign of strength.

The Winning Mindset

Michael Phelps's success came from more than just natural talent. His mindset, discipline, and self-awareness were the key to his greatness.

Laser-Focused Training

Phelps's training routine was legendary. Under Bob Bowman's strict guidance, he trained seven days a week. He swam twice or thrice daily, lifted weights, and followed a high-calorie diet to fuel his workouts. His discipline was unmatched. He showed up every day, even when tired or unmotivated.

He also practiced mental preparation. Before big races, Phelps used visualization techniques, imagining every part of the event from the dive to the final touch. He said he saw himself winning in his mind before he ever stepped onto the starting block.

He once said, "If you want to be the best, you have to do things other people aren't willing to do." That mindset helped him push past physical limits and achieve the impossible.

Commitment to Mental Health

As Phelps matured, he understood that his mental health was as important as his physical condition. After years of battling depression, he became a strong voice for mental health awareness.

He started sharing his story so others wouldn't feel alone. He partnered with organizations like Talkspace to help make therapy more accessible. His message to the world was simple: "It's OK not to be OK. But it's not OK to not get help."

Through treatment and speaking openly, Phelps found balance. He regained his love for swimming and returned to the Olympics one last time in 2016, winning five more golds and a silver. It was a victory not just in the pool, but in life.

Legacy and Impact

Michael Phelps's impact stretches far beyond Olympic records. Through the Michael Phelps Foundation, he teaches kids about water safety, healthy habits, and emotional well-being. His voice has helped open doors for honest conversations about mental health in sports.

Phelps permitted others to do the same by speaking up about his struggles. His story has helped athletes and everyday people understand that reaching out for support is okay.

He proved that greatness isn't just about winning—it's about growing, learning, and helping others.

Lessons for Teens

Michael Phelps's story offers important lessons for teens working through their challenges and dreams:

1. **Channel Your Energy** – Find positive outlets where your energy and focus can help you thrive.

2. **Be Disciplined** – Show up every day and give your best, even when it's hard.

3. **Visualize Success** – Picture your goals clearly and prepare mentally for what you want to achieve.

4. **Take Care of Your Mental Health** – Your emotional well-being matters. Don't be afraid to seek help.

5. **Grow from Setbacks** – Mistakes and struggles don't define you—they teach you how to be stronger.

Swimming Toward Strength

Michael Phelps's story is about more than medals. It's about what happens when someone faces their struggles, gets help, and keeps going. He reminds us that greatness comes not from perfection, but from perseverance.

To young people facing their battles, Phelps's journey is a message of hope: whatever you're going through, you are not alone. And with the right mindset and support, you can achieve more than you ever imagined.

MEGAN RAPINOE

Boldness on the Field and Beyond

Megan Rapinoe is more than a soccer star—she's a force for change. She has secured her place in sports history with two World Cup titles, an Olympic gold medal, and countless honors. But it's not just her skill that sets her apart. Rapinoe has used her platform to stand up for equality, LGBTQ+ rights, and social justice, becoming a symbol of boldness and authenticity. Her story shows how courage can change the world on and off the field.

Early Life and Introduction to Soccer

Megan Anna Rapinoe was born on July 5, 1985, in Redding, California, alongside her fraternal twin sister, Rachael. Their parents encouraged them to stay active and out of trouble, and it didn't take long for both sisters to fall in love with soccer. They spent hours practicing in the backyard and playing on local teams.

By high school, Megan's talent was undeniable. She joined the elite youth club Elk Grove Pride and quickly earned a reputation for her speed, footwork, and smart plays. College recruiters took notice, and she joined the University of Portland, where she helped lead her team to an undefeated season and a national championship in 2005.

Rising to Stardom

In 2009, Rapinoe began her professional career after being drafted into Women's Professional Soccer (WPS). Over the next decade, she became a standout player for the U.S. Women's National Team (USWNT), helping the team win the FIFA Women's World Cup in 2015 and 2019, and earning Olympic gold in 2012.

Her performance at the 2019 World Cup was unforgettable. She won the Golden Boot for top scorer and the Golden Ball for best player. With her arms raised and head held high after scoring, she created a powerful image of confidence and pride that inspired millions.

Overcoming Criticism and Embracing Activism

Despite her success, Rapinoe has faced intense criticism. In 2012, she publicly came out as gay, becoming one of the first high-profile athletes to do so. Some praised her bravery, while others reacted with negativity. Still, Rapinoe never backed down. She proudly lived her truth and became a role model for LGBTQ+ athletes.

In 2016, she drew national attention when she knelt during the national anthem in support of NFL quarterback Colin Kaepernick's protest against police brutality. Many people criticized her, calling her unpatriotic. But Rapinoe stood by her decision. "I will continue to use my platform to fight for what I believe in," she said.

The Winning Mindset

Megan Rapinoe's strength lies not only in her athletic skill but in her powerful mindset. Her career is built on boldness, resilience, and a desire to inspire change.

Boldness

Rapinoe is fearless. On the field, she plays with precision, flair, and confidence. Off the field, she speaks her mind. She never hesitates to take a stand, whether calling out injustice or challenging political leaders.

During the 2019 World Cup, she declined to visit the White House and made headlines by stating, "I'm not going to the [expletive] White House." Her statement sparked controversy, but she stood firm, believing that athletes should hold leaders accountable.

Resilience

Rapinoe has faced injuries, criticism, and backlash, but always comes back stronger. In 2015, she tore her ACL, an injury that could have ended her career. Through intense rehab and hard work, she returned to elite competition. Her strength is more than physical—it's mental.

She stays focused on her goals even when facing negativity for her activism or identity. She has repeatedly shown the world what it means to rise, never giving up on what she believes in.

Inspiring Change

Rapinoe's impact goes far beyond soccer. She has fought for equal pay for female athletes, helped raise awareness about racism and discrimination, and worked closely with social justice organizations. She uses her voice to lift others and push for a fairer world.

In 2019, she and her teammates filed a lawsuit against the U.S. Soccer Federation demanding equal pay and treatment. Rapinoe became a leading voice in the fight, saying, "We're not going to accept anything less."

Legacy and Impact

Megan Rapinoe has left a lasting mark on sports and society. She has redefined what it means to be a champion, not just someone who wins games but uses their platform for good. Her influence stretches beyond soccer fields into schools, communities, and public debates.

She has shown the power of living authentically, speaking out for others, and standing up for what's right. Her example has helped other athletes feel brave enough to do the same.

Lessons for Teens

Megan Rapinoe's journey is filled with lessons for young people who want to make a difference:

1. **Be Bold** – Speak up for what's right, even when difficult.

2. **Stay Resilient** – Turn challenges into strength and keep moving forward.

3. **Embrace Your Identity** – Be proud of who you are. Authenticity is powerful.

4. **Use Your Voice** – You can influence change. Don't be afraid to lead.

5. **Aim for Excellence** – Push yourself to do your best in everything you pursue.

Boldness That Inspires

Megan Rapinoe has shown that being bold, resilient, and true to yourself can change lives. Her courage on the field matches her courage in life. Through soccer and advocacy, she has proven that real champions win trophies and lead change.

To teens everywhere, Rapinoe's story is a reminder that your voice matters, your actions matter, and you can leave a legacy far beyond the scoreboard with bravery and belief.

DEREK REDMOND

Perseverance in the Face of Heartbreak

D erek Redmond will forever be remembered for one of the most emotional and unforgettable moments in Olympic history—not for winning a race, but for refusing to give up. During the 1992 Barcelona Olympic Games, Redmond suffered a painful injury mid-race in the 400-meter semifinal. Yet, instead of quitting, he chose to keep going. With the help of his father, he limped across the finish line, creating a lasting symbol of courage, perseverance, and love.

Early Life and Rise in Athletics

Derek Redmond was born in Bletchley, England, on September 3, 1965. From a young age, it was clear that he had athletic talent. He excelled in several sports, but track and field—especially the 400 meters— captured his focus. With speed, strength, and determination, Redmond rose quickly in British athletics.

He became a top sprinter and a key member of Great Britain's 4x400-meter relay team. In 1985, he broke the British 400-meter record, and in 1991, he helped his team win gold at the World Championships. But his journey was far from smooth. Between 1986 and 1991, Redmond underwent five surgeries on his Achilles tendon. Injuries constantly tested him, yet he kept pushing forward, aiming for Olympic glory.

The 1992 Barcelona Olympics

By the 1992 Olympics, Redmond had fought back into top form. He breezed through the heats and reached the semifinals of the men's 400-meter race. That day was supposed to be his chance to shine.

But halfway through the semifinal, disaster struck. Redmond's hamstring tore, sending him crashing to the ground in agony. As medics rushed toward him, he waved them off. He was in pain, but he wasn't ready to quit. Slowly, he stood up and began hobbling toward the finish line.

Moments later, his father, Jim Redmond, broke through security and ran onto the track to support him. With his father's arm around him, Derek kept going. Step by painful step, they made their way to the finish line, as 65,000 spectators stood and cheered. Though he didn't win the race, Redmond finished it with dignity, strength, and love.

The Winning Mindset

Derek Redmond's story is not about a gold medal—it's about grit. He showed the world that time or trophies don't always measure success. Sometimes, success means refusing to give up, no matter the cost.

Perseverance

Redmond's career was filled with setbacks. Injuries, surgeries, and lost opportunities might have stopped someone else. But Redmond refused to be defined by failure. He once said, "I didn't want to be remembered as the guy who quit. I wanted to finish, no matter what it took."

That mindset carried him through that painful race in Barcelona. He didn't finish first, but he did finish. And in doing so, he showed the world what perseverance looks like.

Courage to Keep Going

What Redmond did on that track took more than physical strength. It took courage. He could have stayed down. No one would have blamed him. But he stood up, kept moving, and finished what he started—even in pain and disappointment.

The image of his father holding him up became a symbol of love and support. In that moment, they reminded the world that it's okay to lean on others, and that courage is often found in the decision to keep going when everything hurts.

Inspiring Others

Derek Redmond's finish became one of the most powerful Olympic moments ever. His determination touched millions. Even without a medal, he became a hero. His story is used in classrooms, speeches, and motivational films to teach people about resilience.

After retiring from athletics, Redmond began sharing his journey with others as a motivational speaker. His message is simple but powerful: you don't have to win to be successful. You have to keep going.

Legacy and Impact

Derek Redmond's Olympic run changed how people define success. He reminded the world that moments of strength often come when everything falls apart. His story motivates people to stay strong during tough times and finish what they start, no matter the challenges.

Redmond built a legacy that goes far beyond sports by turning his pain into purpose. He reminds us that how we respond to setbacks can inspire others to believe in themselves, too.

Lessons for Teens

Derek Redmond's story offers powerful lessons for anyone who's ever felt like giving up:

1. **Finish What You Start** – Even if it's stiff or painful, there's strength in crossing the finish line.

2. **Persevere Through Adversity** – Don't let setbacks stop you. Keep pushing forward.

3. **Lean on Others** – It's okay to ask for help. Support from loved ones makes a difference.

4. **Focus on Effort, Not Outcomes** – It's not always about winning. What matters most is your effort and heart.

5. **Inspire Through Your Actions** – How you face your struggles can give hope to others.

A Race That Will Never Be Forgotten

Derek Redmond didn't leave Barcelona with a medal but went with something far greater. His bravery, refusal to quit, and bond with his father created a legacy that still moves people today. His story proves that true greatness isn't about how fast you run—it's about having the heart to finish the race.

JACKIE ROBINSON

Breaking Barriers with Courage and Grace

J ackie Robinson didn't just play baseball—he changed it forever. When he became the first African-American to play Major League Baseball (MLB) in the modern era, he faced relentless racism, pressure, and hostility. But instead of fighting back with anger, Robinson used strength, patience, and quiet dignity to break barriers and inspire a nation. His journey is one of resilience, leadership, and the power in the face of injustice.

Early Life and Athletic Prowess

Jack Roosevelt Robinson was born in Cairo, Georgia, on January 31, 1919. After his father left the family, Jackie was raised by his mother, Mallie, in Pasadena, California. Growing up in a primarily white neighborhood, he experienced racism at a young age, and it never entirely disappeared from his life.

Robinson had a natural gift for sports. He excelled in baseball, basketball, football, and track at John Muir High School and Pasadena Junior College. At UCLA, he became the first student-athlete in the school's history to earn varsity letters in four sports. However, due to financial struggles, he left college before graduating.

During World War II, Robinson served in the U.S. Army. While stationed in Texas, he refused to move to the back of a segregated bus and was court-martialed. He was later acquitted, a moment that revealed his refusal to accept injustice—something that would define the rest of his life.

Breaking the Color Barrier

In 1945, Robinson joined the Kansas City Monarchs of the Negro Leagues. That same year, Branch Rickey, general manager of the Brooklyn Dodgers, took notice of his talent and strength of character. Rickey wanted a player who could withstand abuse and discrimination without reacting with anger. Robinson said yes when he asked Jackie if he had the courage not to fight back.

Robinson joined the Dodgers' minor league affiliate, the Montreal Royals, and made his MLB debut with the Brooklyn Dodgers on April

15, 1947. That day, he became the first Black player in Major League Baseball in over 60 years.

The Winning Mindset

Robinson's ability to succeed while facing intense racism came from his strong mindset. He showed patience, persevered with dignity, and remained calm under enormous pressure.

Patience

From his first game, Robinson was targeted with insults, threats, and even attempts to injure him. Some of his teammates initially refused to play alongside him. But he didn't react with anger. He kept playing. He let his performance speak louder than any words ever could.

Robinson's patience wasn't a sign of weakness—it was a sign of strength. He knew that losing control would only give his critics what they wanted. So, he stayed focused, played hard, and earned the respect of teammates and fans.

Dignity

Jackie Robinson understood that he wasn't just playing for himself. He was opening doors for others. Everything he did—on and off the field—was with purpose. He carried himself gracefully, knowing how he acted would shape how people saw Black athletes.

In one game against the Philadelphia Phillies, manager Ben Chapman and his team hurled insults at Robinson nonstop. Instead of responding, Robinson stayed focused and helped his team win. His quiet dignity made a powerful statement—one stronger than any insult could match.

After baseball, Robinson continued to lead with integrity. He became a vocal supporter of civil rights, spoke out against injustice, and used his platform to push for equality. Whether in uniform or not, he never stopped fighting for what was right.

Calm Under Pressure

Robinson didn't just survive pressure—he thrived under it. He led the Dodgers to six National League pennants and a World Series win in 1955. He was named Rookie of the Year in 1947 and National League MVP in 1949.

Even during intense moments, Robinson kept his focus. He was known for stealing bases, including home plate—something he did 19 times during his career. These daring moves weren't just athletic—they showed his courage and confidence.

Over time, even skeptical teammates became supporters. Pee Wee Reese famously put his arm around Robinson during a game, a simple act that sent a strong message of unity to the crowd and the country.

Legacy and Impact

Jackie Robinson's legacy stretches far beyond baseball. His courage helped change how people saw race in sports and society. He opened doors for future generations of Black athletes and helped spark conversations about fairness and inclusion.

After retiring from baseball, Robinson continued his fight for justice. He became a business leader and a key figure in the civil rights movement. He served on the board of the NAACP and worked to bring opportunities to underserved communities.

In 1997, MLB honored him by retiring his number, 42, across all teams—a first in professional sports. Every year on April 15, players and fans celebrate Jackie Robinson Day to remember his impact and carry his legacy forward.

Lessons for Teens

Jackie Robinson's life story offers powerful lessons for anyone facing challenges:

1. **Be Patient** – Patience allows you to stay strong when things get tough.

2. **Carry Yourself with Dignity** – Treat others respectfully, even when they don't return it.

3. **Stay Calm Under Pressure** – Stay focused on your goals, no matter the distractions.

4. **Use Your Platform for Good** – Use your voice and actions to help others.

5. **Believe in Yourself** – Trust your abilities and never let others define your worth.

A Hero for Every Generation

Jackie Robinson was more than a great baseball player. He was a leader, a trailblazer, and a symbol of what's possible when strength, courage, and character come together. He didn't just change the game—he changed the country.

Through his story, teens learn that greatness isn't just about talent—how you carry yourself, the values you stand for, and the change you inspire in others. Jackie Robinson proved that true champions rise above, not just for themselves, but for everyone who comes after.

WILMA RUDOLPH

Tenacity and Triumph Against All Odds

Wilma Rudolph showed the world that no obstacle is too significant when matched with determination and heart. Born into poverty and struck with polio as a child, she went from being unable to walk to becoming the fastest woman in the world. At the 1960 Olympics, she made history as the first American woman to win three gold medals in a single Games. Her journey inspires people everywhere to believe in themselves and never give up.

Early Life and Challenges

Wilma Glodean Rudolph was born in Saint Bethlehem, Tennessee, on June 23, 1940. She was the twentieth of twenty-two siblings in a large, loving family. Growing up in the segregated South, Wilma faced many challenges, including limited access to medical care. At four years old, she contracted polio, which weakened her left leg and left her unable to walk without support.

Doctors told her family she might never walk again. But her mother refused to accept that. Wilma slowly gained strength with daily leg massages from her family and regular trips to distant clinics. She wore leg braces for several years, but by age nine, she surprised everyone when she walked without them. Soon, she was playing basketball and running with the other kids—and discovering her love for sports.

Rising Through Adversity

By the time she reached high school, Wilma's athletic talent was evident. She shone on the basketball court and the track, becoming one of the fastest runners in the state. Her speed caught the attention of Ed Temple, coach of the Tennessee State University women's track team. He invited her to train with him during the summers, allowing her to compete with the best.

At sixteen, Wilma competed in the 1956 Melbourne Olympics and won a bronze medal in the 4x100-meter relay. That experience prepared her for something even bigger.

The 1960 Rome Olympics

Wilma Rudolph's shining moment came at the 1960 Olympic Games in Rome. There, she won gold medals in the 100-meter, 200-meter, and 4x100-meter relay events, making her the first American woman to win three golds in a single Olympics. She became an international sensation, hailed as the fastest woman in the world.

But her success wasn't just about winning races. Wilma's triumph symbolized something bigger. She proved that someone who had once been told she would never walk could rise to become the best in the world. Her story broke through barriers of race, gender, and disability and showed people everywhere what was possible with courage and determination.

The Winning Mindset

Wilma Rudolph's strength came from more than her speed. Her mindset—full of determination, faith, and purpose—carried her through the most challenging moments and led her to victory.

Tenacity

Wilma never gave up, no matter what she faced. She met each challenge with steady determination, from polio to poverty to prejudice. She worked hard, trained harder, and refused to let anything stop her.

She once said, "The triumph can't be had without the struggle." For Wilma, every step she took was a reminder of the journey she had traveled. She turned her pain into power and her setbacks into steppingstones.

Faith in Her Ability

One of Wilma's greatest strengths was believing in herself. Even when others doubted her, she knew she had the strength to succeed. Her confidence helped her push past physical limits and mental doubts.

Wilma also leaned on the belief others had in her. Her family, her coach, and her community never stopped encouraging her. That support helped her stay focused and reminded her she wasn't alone in her journey.

Inspiring Others

Wilma Rudolph's victories inspired the world, especially young Black girls who had never seen someone like them win at such a high level. She symbolized hope and strength, showing people they could dream big and succeed.

After retiring from competition, Wilma focused on helping others. She founded the Wilma Rudolph Foundation to support young athletes, and she traveled the world as a goodwill ambassador, spreading messages of determination and equality.

Legacy and Impact

Wilma Rudolph's impact went far beyond the track. She helped change how the world saw women and African-American athletes. Her life symbolized what can happen when someone refuses to quit.

She was an important voice during the civil rights movement and always insisted on being treated with respect. After returning home from the Olympics, she refused to attend a celebration in her honor unless it was integrated, marking her hometown's first racially integrated event.

Wilma's story inspires generations of athletes, activists, and dreamers. She showed that greatness isn't about where you start, but how far you're willing to go.

Lessons for Teens

Wilma Rudolph's life teaches powerful lessons to young people facing their challenges:

1. **Never Give Up** – Keep moving forward even when the odds seem impossible.

2. **Believe in Yourself** – Trust your abilities and hold on to your dreams.

3. **Find Strength in Support** – Surround yourself with people who lift you.

4. **Turn Struggles into Triumphs** – Let your challenges make you stronger.

5. **Inspire Others** – Use your story to give others hope.

A Legacy of Strength

Wilma Rudolph turned pain into purpose and setbacks into milestones. From a small girl with leg braces to the world's fastest woman, she became a living symbol of determination and grace.

Her story reminds us all that no matter where we start or what we face, we have the power to rise, run, and leave a lasting impact on the world.

SERENA WILLIAMS

A Champion's Mindset

S erena Williams became one of the greatest athletes in history through talent, perseverance, and an unstoppable spirit. Born in a tough neighborhood, she rose above the noise—literally and figuratively—to dominate the tennis world. Serena didn't just play tennis. She changed the game.

The Early Years

Serena Jameka Williams was born in Saginaw, Michigan, on September 26, 1981. When she was still young, her family moved to Compton, California, a place known for gang violence and poverty. She was the youngest of five sisters, and her family stayed close and supportive.

Serena's father, Richard Williams, and her mother, Oracene Price, saw early potential in Serena and her older sister, Venus. Richard believed in them so much that he became their coach. He trained them hard, often on cracked public courts in Compton. Despite the challenging environment, Serena never gave up. Gunshots were sometimes heard during practice, but she kept swinging her racket. She learned to stay focused, no matter what was happening around her.

"Tennis was my escape," Serena later said. "It was a way to rise above my circumstances and dream of a brighter future."

Facing Racism and Sexism in Tennis

As Serena got better and began playing in junior tournaments, she faced more than just tough opponents. She dealt with racism and sexism in a sport long dominated by wealthy, white athletes. Some people didn't want to accept a strong, confident Black girl on the court.

In 2001, during the Indian Wells tournament, the crowd booed Serena throughout the final. Her family also faced ugly, racist remarks. It was one of the most challenging moments in her career. Serena didn't return to Indian Wells for over ten years. But instead of quitting, she used that pain to push herself further. She turned hate into strength.

"Being underestimated or criticized has always turned into opportunities for growth," Serena said. "It made me stronger."

The Winning Mindset

Serena's strength doesn't just come from her muscles. Her most considerable power is her mindset. Her deep confidence, tireless work ethic, and belief in herself helped her rise above challenges that could have broken others.

Unshakable Confidence

Even as a young girl, Serena believed she would be great. She wasn't arrogant—she just trusted herself. This inner belief gave her the courage to take risks and push through pressure.

One powerful example came during the 2015 French Open. Serena was down in a tough match against Victoria Azarenka but didn't panic. She stayed calm, fought back with powerful shots, and won the game—and eventually the whole tournament. Her focus under pressure showed how much she trusted herself.

Serena's confidence also shows up off the court. She speaks out for women's rights and racial justice. She's proud of her body and wants others to feel the same. "What my body achieves makes me proud," she said. "And I want every woman to feel that."

Relentless Work Ethic

Serena's success wasn't handed to her—it was earned through hard work. From long hours of practice in the California heat to grueling workouts as a pro, Serena always pushed herself. She didn't just rely on talent. She trained harder than anyone else.

Her coach, Patrick Mouratoglou, once said, "Her work ethic remains unmatched." Even after becoming the best, Serena kept working to get better. She never settled.

In 2017, Serena gave birth to her daughter, Olympia. Just months later, she was back on the court, competing against the best in the world. Balancing motherhood and professional sports isn't easy, but Serena did it with strength and determination.

Belief in Her Potential

Serena never stopped believing in herself, not when she was doubted, injured, or facing personal struggles. That belief carried her through the most challenging moments.

When she returned to tennis after becoming a mom, many people thought she was done. But Serena didn't listen. She made it to four Grand Slam finals between 2018 and 2019. She kept going because she believed in her journey. As she said often, "I'm not done yet."

A Legacy of Greatness

Serena's impact goes far beyond the 23 Grand Slam singles titles she won. She inspired a new generation—especially girls and young athletes of color—to dream big and fight for their goals. She showed that greatness is about more than trophies. It's about heart, courage, and determination.

Off the court, Serena gives back. She supports charities and speaks up for what's right. She broke barriers and made the tennis world and the world a better place. Serena isn't just a tennis champion. She's a champion for change.

Lessons for Teens

Serena Williams's journey teaches us powerful lessons. Here are five takeaways for young people:

1. **Turn Hardship into Strength** - Don't let challenges stop you. Use them to grow stronger.

2. **Believe in Yourself** - Confidence starts with believing in your potential, even if others don't.

3. **Work Hard and Stay Focused** - Success comes from discipline and effort, not shortcuts.

4. **Be Resilient** - Everyone faces setbacks. The key is bouncing back and never giving up.

5. **Lift Others** - Use your success to inspire and support those around you.

Serena Williams proved that where you start doesn't define where you can go. Her grit, passion, and belief in herself helped her breakthrough every barrier. She didn't just win matches—she won hearts, too.

TIGER WOODS

Focus, Resilience,
and the Power of Rebuilding

Tiger Woods is more than just a famous golfer. His life is a story of focus, strength, and the courage to rebuild. He became one of the greatest athletes in history with 15 major championships and 82 PGA Tour victories. But Tiger's journey wasn't just about winning—it was about pushing through pain, bouncing back from setbacks, and never giving up on himself.

Early Life and the Challenge of Racism

Eldrick Tont Woods, better known as Tiger Woods, was born in Cypress, California, on December 30, 1975. His father, Earl Woods, was a retired Army officer and an amateur golfer. Tiger's dad introduced him to golf when he was just two years old, and it quickly became clear he was something special.

By age eight, Tiger had already won his first Junior World Golf Championship—a title he would win multiple times. But even as he collected trophies, Tiger faced racism. His biracial background—Black from his father's side and Thai, Chinese, and Dutch from his mother's—often made him a target. He heard hurtful words at country clubs and junior tournaments and felt like he didn't belong.

Tiger later shared, "The world has called me names." But instead of letting those words break him, he turned them into fuel. He became stronger, more focused, and more determined to prove himself.

Dominating the World of Golf

After playing college golf at Stanford University, Tiger turned pro in 1996. A year later, he shocked the world by winning the Masters. At just 21 years old, he became the youngest golfer ever to win that major, and he did it by a record-breaking 12 strokes.

Tiger's powerful swing and calm under pressure changed the sport forever. He didn't just play the game—he redefined it. For over 10 years, he was nearly unbeatable. He became world number one for a record 683 weeks and won all four major titles in a row, a feat known as the "Tiger Slam."

Tough Times: Injuries and Personal Struggles

Tiger's path wasn't always smooth. He faced serious challenges that tested every part of him—physically, emotionally, and mentally.

Injuries

Tiger's aggressive playing style took a toll on his body. He had multiple surgeries on his knees, back, and Achilles tendon. Yet he pushed through the pain. In 2008, he won the U.S. Open while playing with a torn ACL and stress fractures in his leg. That win showed just how tough he was.

But by 2015, after many injuries, people began to wonder if Tiger's golf career was over.

Personal Scandals

In 2009, Tiger's personal life fell apart when news broke of his extramarital affairs. His marriage ended, and his reputation took a huge hit. Sponsors dropped him, and fans turned away. Tiger stepped back from golf for a while, unsure if he'd ever return.

It was one of the lowest points in his life.

The Winning Mindset

What makes Tiger Woods truly special is his ability to return from failure. His mental toughness, intense focus, and belief in second chances helped him fight his way back.

Laser-Sharp Focus

Tiger is known for his focus. On the course, nothing distracts him. He studies each hole, each shot, and each opponent with total concentration.

A shining example came during the 2008 U.S. Open. On the 18th hole, in pain and needing a birdie to stay in the game, he sank a 12-foot putt under pressure. He went on to win the playoff the next day, even though he could barely walk.

Tiger's focus goes beyond the game. He prepares like few others—mentally, physically, and strategically. He wants every advantage, and he earns it through study and practice.

Unbreakable Resilience

Tiger's story is filled with comebacks. No matter how often he was knocked down, he always got back up—stronger than before.

After spinal fusion surgery in 2017, many believed Tiger would never win again. But in 2019, at age 43, he stunned the world by winning the Masters. Fans cried. Even his competitors cheered. It was one of the greatest comebacks in sports history.

He once said, "Winning takes care of everything." For Tiger, success was never about being perfect but rising after falling.

Belief in Rebuilding

Tiger never lost belief in himself. Even when his body failed him and the world criticized him, he held onto the hope that he could rebuild.

After his 2019 Masters win, Tiger spoke about the importance of perseverance. He reminded everyone that even when life feels broken, there's always a way back. With effort, focus, and time, anyone can rebuild.

That belief made Tiger more than a champion—it made him a role model.

A Lasting Legacy

Tiger's impact goes far beyond the golf course. He brought millions of new fans to the sport. He inspired kids of all backgrounds to pick up a club and dream big. Golf became more diverse and competitive because of him.

Of course, Tiger started the TGR Foundation to help students from underserved communities access quality education. He believes in giving back and lifting others.

Lessons for Teens

Tiger Woods's journey teaches young people that greatness doesn't mean never falling but learning how to rise again.

Here are five powerful lessons:

1. **Stay Focused** - Clear goals and strong focus help you push through distractions and challenges.

2. **Be Resilient** - Tough times will come, but your strength grows when you keep going anyway.

3. **Believe in Second Chances** - Mistakes don't define you. What matters is how you rebuild.

4. **Keep Working Hard** - Talent helps, but dedication and effort build real success.

5. **Grow from Adversity** - Hard moments can teach you the most. Use them to grow stronger.

Tiger Woods's life is a story of highs and lows, glory and pain. But through it all, he showed what's possible when someone keeps believing in their dreams. He didn't let failure stop him. Instead, he proved that a true champion always finds a way to rise even after falling hard.

www.ingramcontent.com/pod-product-compliance
Lightning Source LLC
Chambersburg PA
CBHW061655120626
46550CB00003B/953